Face to Face

POLAR ANIMALS

Q2A Media

Created by Q2A Media
www.q2amedia.com
Text, design & illustrations Copyright © 2007 Q2A Media

Editor Honor Head
Publishing Director Chester Fisher
Creative Director Simmi Sikka
Senior Designers Rahul Dhiman and Joita Das

Illustrators Subhash Vohra, Aadil A Siddiqui, and Amit Tayal
Art Editor Sujatha Menon
Picture Researcher Lalit Dalal

Tangerine Press edition Copyright © 2007 Scholastic Inc.

an imprint of
SCHOLASTIC
www.scholastic.com

Scholastic and Tangerine Press and associated logos are trademarks of Scholastic Inc.

Published by Tangerine Press, an imprint of Scholastic Inc.,
557 Broadway; New York, NY 10012

Scholastic New Zealand Ltd.
Greenmount, Auckland

Scholastic Canada Ltd.
Markham, Ontario

Scholastic Australia Pty. Ltd
Gosford NSW

Scholastic UK
Coventry, Warwickshire

10 9 8 7 6 5 4 3 2 1

ISBN-10: 0-545-02563-X
ISBN-13: 978-0-545-02563-8

Printed in India

Picture Credits

Cover Images:
Front Anthony Hathaway.
Back Steve Estvanik.

8b Dan Guravich: Oxford Scientific Films: Photolibrary. **8t** Terry W. Eggers: Corbis. **10** Bruemmer Fred: Peter Arnold Images Inc: Photolibrary. **11t** Hinrich Baesemann: DPA. **11b** Andrewartha Gary & Terry: Oxford Scientific Films: Photolibrary. **12** Douglas Smith: NPS. **13t** Alaska Stock Images. **13b** Robert Winslow Photography: Photographersdirect.com. **14t** Alaska Stock Images. **14b** Erwin & Peggy Bauer: Animals Animals: Earth Scenes: Photolibrary. **16** Pete Cairns: Nature Picture Library. **17t** Tom Mangelsen: Nature Picture Library. **18-19** Peter Bassett: Nature Picture Library. **19t** Doug Allan: Nature Picture Library. **20t** Aflo: Nature Picture Library. **20b** Photo Researchers, Inc: Photolibrary. **22b** Mats Forsberg: Nature Picture Library. **22-23** Doug Allan: Oxford Scientific Films: Photolibrary. **23t** John Beatty: Science Photo Library: Photolibrary. **24** Seapics.com. **26-27t** Richard Ellis: Photo Researchers, Inc: Photolibrary. **26-27b** DIA Contact: Sunset. **27** Doug Allan: Oxford Scientific Films: Photolibrary. **29** Seapics.com. **30-31t** Paul Souders: Corbis. **30b** Frans Lanting: Minden Pictures. **32-33** Daniel Cox: Photolibrary. **32b** William Ervin: Science Photo Library: Photolibrary. **33t** Pete Oxford: Nature Picture Library. **34b** Jose Schell: Nature Picture Library. **34-35m** Seapics.com. **35t** Fotolibra. **36t** Daniel Cox: Oxford Scientific Films: Photolibrary. **36b** Eric and David Hosking: Corbis. **37t** WorldFoto: Alamy. **37b** Richard Packwood: Oxford Scientific Films: Photolibrary. **38t** Daniel J. Cox: Corbis. **38b** Canadian Museum of Nature. **40** Seapics.com. **40-41b** Arctic-Images: Corbis. **41t** Sutton-Hibbert: Rex Features. **42b** Graham Neden: Ecoscene. **42-43t** Dan Guravich: Corbis. **43** NASA

POLAR ANIMALS

SALLY MORGAN

tangerine
press

an imprint of

SCHOLASTIC

Contents

polar bear

Greenland shark

penguins

harp seal

Life at the Poles

There are many animals that live in some of the harshest conditions on Earth. They survive freezing temperatures, months of darkness, and strong, howling winds. These animals live in the polar regions.

Long, cold winters

The Arctic and the Antarctic have dark, bleak winters. The Sun sinks below the horizon and does not reappear for several months. In the Antarctic, temperatures fall to about −94°F (−70°C), and strong winds make it feel even colder. In summer, the temperatures creep up to just above freezing, and the Sun shines all day and night.

 *Penguins, such as these Adelies, rest on icebergs that have broken away from the Antarctic ice sheet. In some places, the ice sheet is 10,000 feet (3,000 m) thick. There are about 17 kinds of penguins in the world. Of these only four live in Antarctica.*

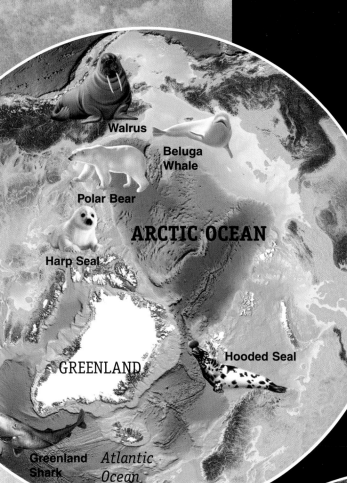

Walrus

Beluga Whale

Polar Bear

ARCTIC OCEAN

Harp Seal

Hooded Seal

GREENLAND

Greenland Shark

Atlantic Ocean

Extreme survival

Most polar animals are not found anywhere else on Earth. They include the polar bear of the Arctic and the emperor penguin of the Antarctic. Living at very low temperatures is risky for animals as their bodies can freeze and food is difficult to find. Polar animals have many ways of staying warm and surviving the long, cruel winters.

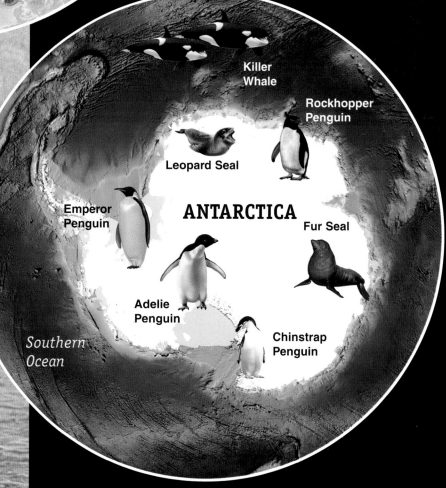

Killer Whale

Rockhopper Penguin

Leopard Seal

ANTARCTICA

Emperor Penguin

Fur Seal

Adelie Penguin

Chinstrap Penguin

Southern Ocean

The Arctic is a frozen ocean at the North Pole, surrounded by land. Antarctica is a huge continent at the South Pole, surrounded by the Southern Ocean.

The Mighty Bear

The polar bear is one of the best-known polar animals. It might look cuddly, but it is a fierce hunter with strong teeth and razorlike claws.

Polar bears can overheat during the summer. When this happens, they lie on the ice to cool down.

FACT

A mother teaches her cubs to swim. Polar bears doggy-paddle with their large paws. Their paws are slightly webbed so they can swim better.

Keeping warm

The polar bear is the largest land predator in the world. A male is 9 feet (3 m) long and weighs up to 1,432 pounds (650 kg). It has thick fur to trap heat. Under its skin is a layer of fat, called blubber, which helps to keep its body warm. A polar bear has thick, white fur, but its skin is black to help it absorb heat from the Sun.

Life on the ice

During the winter, polar bears spend many months hunting seals on the ice, traveling as much as 12 miles (20 km) a day. Polar bears are excellent swimmers and can swim for several hours from one piece of ice to another. When the temperatures rise in early summer, the ice sheet breaks up and the polar bear moves onto land.

Small ears lose less heat than large ears.

Polar bears have a black tongue.

The polar bear uses its long canine teeth to hold its prey. Polar bears do not chew their food, but tear off large chunks which they swallow whole.

Fur is white, but can become yellow.

Long, sharp claws help the polar bear to grip the slippery ice.

The polar bear has fur on the soles of its feet so they do not get cold.

The search for food

Polar bears are powerful predators that may attack animals much larger than themselves. Their favorite food is seal, but they also catch beluga whales, fish, birds, and musk oxen. They can smell a dead seal on the ice from several hundred miles away.

Last breath

Polar bears are cunning hunters. They know that seals and small whales have to come to the surface of the water to breathe. They sit by holes in the ice and wait for a seal or whale to come to the surface.

FACT

Polar bears spend half their time hunting seals.

When a seal or whale pokes its head though the ice, the polar bear will grab it and drag it out.

Giving birth

In the autumn, the female polar bear digs a hole in the ice, called a den, where she spends the winter. During this time, she gives birth to one or two cubs. The cubs are ready to leave the den in spring. The mother breaks through the ice and snow surrounding the den, and the cubs see daylight for the first time.

The cubs follow their mother as she hunts for food. She will attack any other animal that comes too close.

Growing up

Polar bear cubs stay with their mother for up to two years. During this time, the mother teaches them how to hunt. As they get older, the cubs play and have pretend fights. Polar bears live for about 15 to 18 years in the wild.

Teenage cubs have mock fights which help to prepare them for adulthood.

Predators and Prey

Wolves, wolverines, and Arctic foxes are the top predators in the Arctic.

Pack hunters

The gray wolf lives in a group called a pack, which is made up of from two to 20 wolves. The top male and the top female wolf lead the pack. By working together in a pack, a group of wolves can kill an animal, such as a bison or caribou, that is much larger than themselves.

One animal is separated from the herd where it is easier to attack.

The pack surround the animal and pull it to the ground using their sharp teeth and claws.

Arctic fox

During the winter months, the Arctic fox has a white coat to match the snow. In spring, the snow melts and the fox grows a new coat that is blue-gray. Arctic foxes prey on small mammals such as lemmings, as well as birds and their eggs. They are scavengers, too, feeding on the remains of polar bear kills.

▶| *Arctic foxes creep up on small animals, then pounce. They jump 20 inches (50 cm) into the air and come down on the animal from above. They pin the animal to the ground and kill it by biting it through the neck.*

Powerful wolverine

The wolverine is only about the size of a big dog, such as a German Shepherd, but is strong enough to pull down large prey, like caribou and moose. The wolverine jumps onto the back of its prey and holds on with its claws until the animal falls to the ground.

The wolverine's powerful jaws can break the largest bones.

Plant Eaters

The Arctic is home to many plant-eating mammals. The largest are the musk oxen and caribou.

The long journey

Every year, huge herds of caribou leave the sheltered forests where they spend the winter and travel many miles to the vast, treeless tundra where they spend the summer. In winter, the tundra is covered in snow, but in summer, the snow melts, and low-growing plants provide food for the caribou.

Keeping warm

Musk oxen live in herds. During the summer, they feed on plants such as cotton grass, willow, and sedge. They build up a thick layer of fat under their skin which helps to keep them warm. There is little food in winter, so they use their store of fat as food. Musk oxen have long, thick, shaggy hair that protects them in fierce blizzards.

When musk oxen are attacked by wolves, they form a circle around their calves. They face out, forming a barrier with their sharp horns.

A male musk ox may weigh as much as 772 pounds (350 kg). Its large hump makes it look even bigger.

Both male and female musk oxen have horns, although the male's horns are larger.

Their hooves have sharp edges, which help them to move swiftly through snow and ice.

Caribou or reindeer?

In Europe and Asia, the caribou is called the reindeer. However, there are very few wild reindeer. Today, Arctic people keep many herds of reindeer. They stay with their herds all year round, following the reindeer as they walk across the tundra in search of food. The reindeer supply them with meat and skin for clothing.

▶ *Each year a reindeer sheds its antlers and grows new ones. Older males have the biggest antlers.*

Arctic hares are also called snowshoe hares because of their extra-large feet. Their "snowshoes" help them to run across the snow very quickly.

On the lookout

Arctic hares live in the Arctic all year round. In winter, their coat changes color from brown to white. They are hunted by animals such as lynx, bears, wolves, and birds of prey. When there is danger, they stand up on their hind legs so they can decide in which direction to run.

Food for winter

The lemming is less than 5 inches (13 cm) long. It is covered with long, soft fur, which changes color from brown in summer to white in winter. This makes it difficult for predators, such as the snowy owl, to see them. Lemmings feed on roots, leaves, berries, and seeds.

▶| Lemmings live in tunnels under the snow in winter. The snow traps heat in the ground so they stay warm.

FACT

Huge groups of lemmings in search of food run across fields and through towns and villages. If they reach a river, they jump in and try to swim to the other side. Some survive, but many drown.

Masters of the Polar Seas

Seals are expert swimmers with flippers instead of legs and a body that glides easily through the icy waters.

Elephant seals on guard

Each year, elephant seals return to the beaches where they were born. The males arrive first and fight each other to claim as much of the beach as possible. Then the females arrive to give birth to their pups. Each male guards the females on their bit of the beach, fighting off any other male who comes near. Each male guards about 30 to 50 females, but, occasionally, a large male will guard as many as 300 females.

Hooded seal

The hooded seal gets it name from the red balloon it blows up to attract females. The balloon is the lining of one of its nostrils and comes out of its nose.

When the hooded seal shakes its head, the balloon makes a pinging sound.

▼ When two male elephant seals meet on the beach, they rear up, making a lot of threatening noise. Then they fight by smashing their head and neck against each other.

Harp seals

There are millions of harp seals in the Arctic. In spring, the female harp seals gather on the ice to give birth to their pups. The pups grow very quickly. By the time they are 14 days old, they are ready to leave their mother.

Walrus

The walrus is a large seal. It looks very fierce with its long, white tusks, which are strong and sharp. Walruses haul themselves onto the ice with their tusks. Male walruses use their tusks to fight off other males.

⊼ *Harp seal pups are born with white fur and are nicknamed "whitecoats." They lose this white fur within a few weeks, and it is replaced by gray fur.*

⊼ *Walruses can get too hot in the Sun. When this happens, their skin turns pink.*

Walruses live in murky water where they cannot see much. They use their sensitive whiskers to find food on the sea floor.

A walrus can make a lot of different noises, including whistles, barks, grunts, growls, snorts, and coughs.

Tusks are extra-long teeth. Some larger male walruses can have tusks 3 feet (1 m) in length.

Walrus skin is pale gray-brown when the animal comes out of the water.

They use their front flippers to raise their body off the ground.

Dangerous leopard seal

The leopard seal is a strong swimmer that hunts penguins and crabeater seals. It has powerful jaws and long, sharp teeth that slice through meat. It is called a leopard seal because of the black spots on its throat.

Crabeater seal

Crabeater seals do not eat crabs—their favorite food is krill. These seals have small, pointed teeth that fit together to make a sort of strainer. When they take in mouthfuls of water, it drains out through their teeth, leaving the tiny krill behind.

⋏ *The leopard seal swims along the edge of the ice waiting for penguins to come into the water. Then it quickly catches one in its wide jaws.*

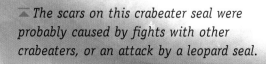

⋏ *The scars on this crabeater seal were probably caused by fights with other crabeaters, or an attack by a leopard seal.*

Sea bear

Fur seals have extra-thick fur, which makes them look a little like a small bear. Fur seals spend the winter at sea and come onto land to give birth to their pups. The females feed their pups for 17 weeks, and then all the seals return to the water.

This fur seal warns off some emperor penguins. Fur seals can move quickly on land because their back flippers point forward and push their body with great power.

FACT

Antarctic fur seals were nearly wiped out by fur hunters. A few survived on some remote islands and were protected, and, gradually, their numbers increased.

Giants of the Sea

Whales are the biggest animals living in the ocean. They spend their entire life in water even though they have to breathe air.

Killer whales

The killer whales, or orcas, are often called the "wolves of the sea" because they hunt together and share the food that they catch. They are fearless hunters, catching fish, squid, seals, and penguins.

Most whales will leap out of the water backward and come down with a big splash. This is called breaching.

Humpback whales

Humpback whales are only seen in polar waters during the summer months. Then they swim to warmer waters where they give birth to their calves. A newborn humpback calf is about 16 feet (5 m) long. It is called a humpback because of the shape it makes as it arches its back in a dive.

All whales have a small hole on the back of their head called a blowhole. When they come to the surface to breathe, they breathe out all the air from their lungs. This creates a spout of bubbles.

Whales use their dorsal fin to help them turn, steer, and stay upright.

Orcas are easily recognized by the white marks near their eyes and on their belly.

A killer whale has between 40 and 52 cone-shaped teeth. Their teeth curve backward to stop prey, such as fish, from slipping out of the whale's mouth.

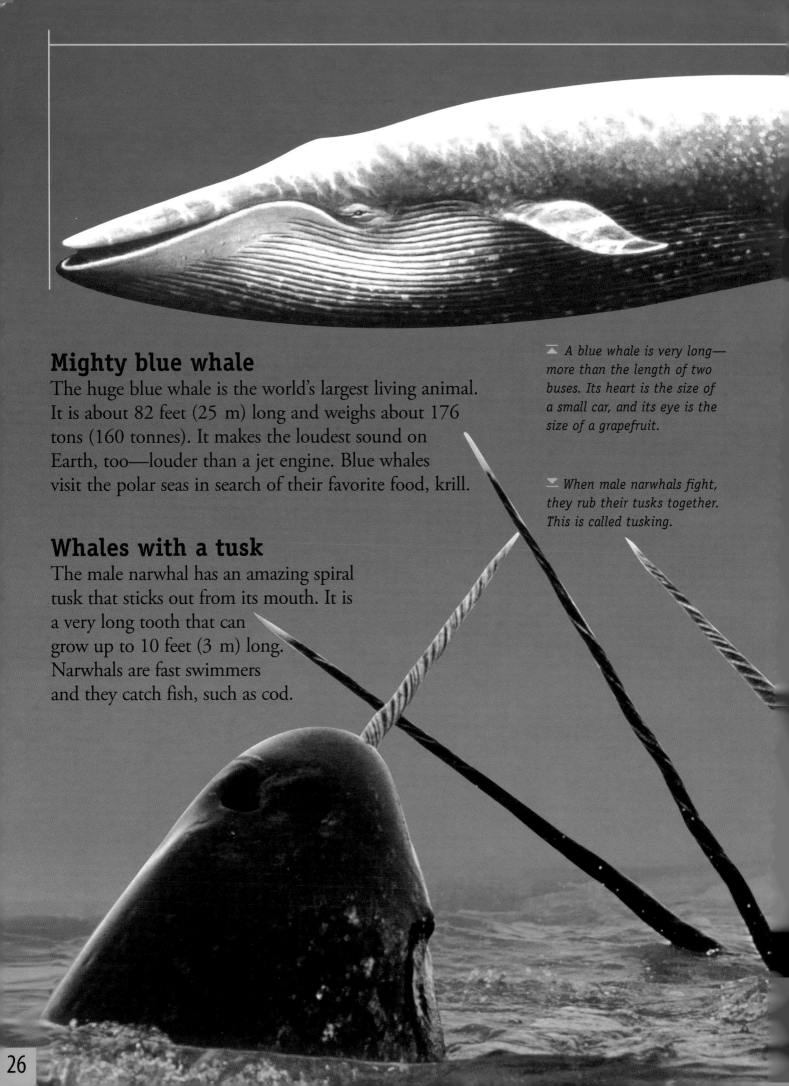

Mighty blue whale

The huge blue whale is the world's largest living animal. It is about 82 feet (25 m) long and weighs about 176 tons (160 tonnes). It makes the loudest sound on Earth, too—louder than a jet engine. Blue whales visit the polar seas in search of their favorite food, krill.

Whales with a tusk

The male narwhal has an amazing spiral tusk that sticks out from its mouth. It is a very long tooth that can grow up to 10 feet (3 m) long. Narwhals are fast swimmers and they catch fish, such as cod.

A blue whale is very long— more than the length of two buses. Its heart is the size of a small car, and its eye is the size of a grapefruit.

When male narwhals fight, they rub their tusks together. This is called tusking.

94 ft (28 m)

6 ft (1.8 m)

White whales

The beluga is a white whale, but its calves are born brown. Their color changes from brown to gray and finally to white by the time the calf is one year old. Beluga whales visit the Arctic, where they catch fish and pick up crabs from the seabed.

▷ *A pod, or group, of beluga work together to hunt fish. When the beluga find a shoal of fish, they will herd the fish into shallow water, where they are easier to catch.*

FACT

Unlike other whales, beluga whales have a neck so they can turn their head sideways.

Polar Sharks

Most sharks are found in warm water, but a few swim into the icy waters of the Arctic. Only one shark spends its whole life under the Arctic ice.

Nearly all Greenland sharks have a small animal called a copepod living on their eye.

Greenland shark

The little-known Greenland shark is rarely seen because they live so deep in the ocean. They mostly swim at depths of 1,312 to 1,968 feet (400 to 600 m), but sometimes they dive as deep as 6,562 feet (2,000 m). The Greenland is bigger than all other sharks except for the great white. It grows to more than 19½ feet (6 m) long.

Sharks have lots of rows of small teeth. When a tooth falls out, it is replaced by a new tooth. Shark teeth have incredibly sharp, jagged edges.

Sharks use their strong tails to help push them through the water.

A shark's skin is covered in a layer of rough scales. If prey touches the skin, the prey can be damaged, which helps the shark to catch it.

The copepod feeds on the Greenland shark's eye and causes it to become semi-blind. In return, the copepod makes its own light that attracts fish to the shark for it to eat.

FACT

Sharks need oxygen to stay alive. As a shark swims, water rushes over its gills. The gills filter oxygen from the water.

▶ *The blue shark visits the Arctic in the summer where it feeds mostly on squid, but it will bite into anything!*

Super senses

Sharks use their senses to find their way around. Their strongest sense is smell, and they can smell tiny amounts of blood in the deepest oceans. They can also pick up vibrations in the water caused by the movements of other animals.

Meet the Penguins

Penguins are birds that cannot fly and have flippers instead of wings. Most of the world's penguins are found in the Antarctic.

Flying in water

Penguins spend many months each year in the icy polar sea. Some of the time they float on the surface of the water and the rest of the time they dive for fish. Penguins "fly" through the water with their flippers held out at each side like wings. They zoom through the water after food.

Surviving the blizzards

Blizzards with violent winds and thick, swirling snow are common in the Antarctic. Some of the worst blizzards can last a week. Penguins huddle close together to keep each other warm.

These young emperor penguins are in a huddle. Those on the outside slowly move into the inside, where it is warmest.

Emperor penguins push themselves through the water by moving their flippers and using their tail to steer. They hold their legs close to their body so they can swim faster.

Thick feathers and blubber help penguins to stay warm in the extreme cold.

With their short legs and large feet, penguins find it difficult to walk. They waddle from side to side very slowly.

Their flippers help them to keep their balance and to swim.

For penguins, it is easier and faster to toboggan down a slope on their front than to walk.

▲ *Adelies jump
into the water from
rocks and icebergs.*

Crowded rookeries

Penguins lay their eggs on land. The place where they gather is called a rookery and can have hundreds of thousands of penguins. Rookeries are noisy places as the penguins call to each other, trying to find their way to their egg.

The adult gentoo penguin spends the day at sea feeding and then coughs up the fish in its stomach to feed its chick.

Emperor penguin

The emperor penguin has a tough life. It has to walk 62 miles (100 km) or so inland to breed. The female lays one egg, which she passes to the male. She then walks back to the sea to feed while the male looks after the egg for the next two months. The male does not eat until the female returns.

▲ *Penguins, such as this emperor penguin, can make big leaps out of the water onto land, especially if they are being chased by a leopard seal!*

Adelies

Adelies are the smallest of the Antarctic penguin, at just 27 inches (70 cm) high. They gather on some of the few ice-free beaches where they build nests from stone. They have to be on guard as other adelies will try to steal the stones for their own nest.

Polar **Birds**

The icy waters of the polar seas are rich in food such as fish, krill, and squid, attracting many types of seabirds.

Breeding colonies

Large colonies of seabirds, such as kittiwakes, puffins, and gannets, live on the coastal cliffs around the icy seas where they are safe from predators, such as foxes. Most do not make a nest, but lay their eggs on narrow ledges on the cliffs.

Hundreds of gannets gather together on a cliffside to lay their eggs. Each female gannet will lay only one egg at a time.

The puffin feeds mostly on a type of small fish called sand eels. It picks up a beakful then carries it back to feed to its chicks.

The puffin's beak is designed to hold a lot of fish at the same time. The average is 10 fish, but the record is 62!

The long, sharp-edged beak of the albatross ends in a hook, which is ideal for catching fish.

Gliding over the ocean

The albatross is one of the world's largest seabirds. It flies effortlessly over the ocean with hardly a beat of its wings. It uses its long, narrow wings to catch the wind to soar up into the air and then glide down again. It dives down to the water to scoop up fish and squid in its hooked beak. The albatross spends much of the year at sea, circling the world many times over. It only returns to land to nest.

The albatross has a wingspan of more than 9 feet (3 m), the longest of any bird.

Many birds, such as these swans, just visit the Arctic, where they nest and raise their young.

Eider ducks

The eider duck spends the summer in the Arctic, feeding on crabs and mussels in the shallow water by the coast. *Eider* is an Icelandic word, which describes the bird's soft, downy feathers. These small feathers are very fluffy and keep the bird warm.

▼ *This king eider duck is a drake (male). The female has plain brown feathers all over.*

Scavenging skuas

Skuas are the pirates of the bird world. They attack other birds, such as gulls and terns, and make them drop any fish they have caught so they can steal it. Skuas are scavengers, too, and will feed on the dead bodies of birds. Some of the larger skuas will even attack and kill adult birds.

⏶ *Skuas will go into nesting colonies looking for eggs and young chicks to snatch.*

Arctic tern

Each year, the Arctic tern makes a record-breaking journey from the Arctic to the Antarctic and back again. The bird spends the summer in the Arctic where it breeds. Then it flies south to Europe and down the coast of Africa or South America to the Antarctic, where it spends the rest of the year. This round-the-world journey is about 21,000 miles (35,000 km) in length.

Arctic terns spend nearly all of their life in the air. They are able to swoop down and pick fish out of the water without getting wet.

Swift and deadly

Snowy owls can have up to seven chicks to feed. The parents fly low over the tundra, hunting for small animals, such as lemmings and voles, moving on the ground. Once they spot their prey, they dive down with talons outstretched to grab the animal. Most owls hunt at night, but the snowy owl hunts day and night. They carry food back to the nest where the female tears it into bits for the chicks.

Birds of Prey

Birds of prey have two main weapons—a vicious hooked beak and sharp, curved talons —which they use to catch birds and small mammals.

Gyrfalcon

The gyrfalcon is the largest falcon in the world. It grows to about 23 inches (60 cm) long and has a wingspan of up to 51 inches (130 cm). It is a powerful bird that flies low and fast when it is chasing prey, such as small birds and lemmings.

▼ The gyrfalcon builds its nest on ledges of cliffs. The parent bird carries prey back to the nest. It uses its hooked beak to pull off small pieces of meat, which it feeds to its chicks.

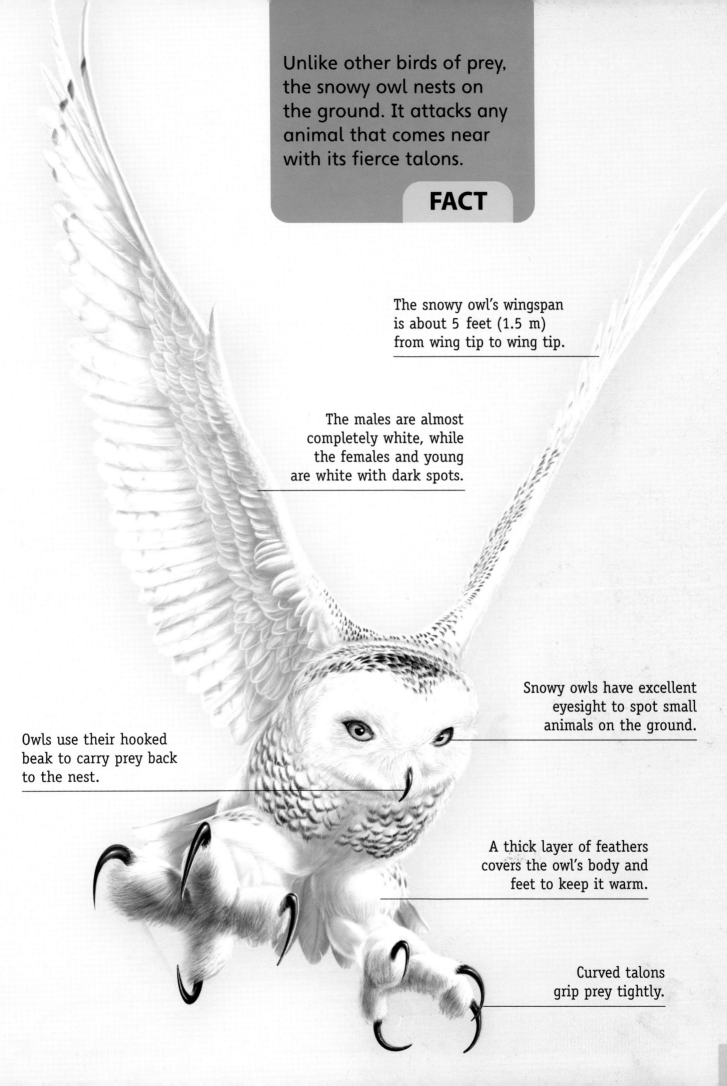

Unlike other birds of prey, the snowy owl nests on the ground. It attacks any animal that comes near with its fierce talons.

FACT

The snowy owl's wingspan is about 5 feet (1.5 m) from wing tip to wing tip.

The males are almost completely white, while the females and young are white with dark spots.

Snowy owls have excellent eyesight to spot small animals on the ground.

Owls use their hooked beak to carry prey back to the nest.

A thick layer of feathers covers the owl's body and feet to keep it warm.

Curved talons grip prey tightly.

The **Future** of **Polar Animals**

The polar regions are among the few places on Earth that remain almost untouched by people. However, many polar animals are threatened because of people in other parts of the world.

Rich polar seas

The polar seas are full of krill and fish, which are vital food supplies for seals, penguins, and whales. Unfortunately, fishing vessels are catching so many fish that the survival of many types of fish is threatened. This means the polar animals do not have the food they need. To stop this, limits can be placed on the amount of fish that can be caught each year.

◄ *The numbers of cod in the ocean has fallen greatly in recent years. Many people think that fishing for cod should stop before this fish disappears completely.*

Whaling

In the past, whales were hunted for their oil and meat. So many were killed that some whale species were at risk of disappearing completely. Then whaling was banned and the numbers of whales increased. Sadly, some countries, such as Japan and Norway, want to start whaling again.

▲ Greenpeace is an international organization. For many years it has protested against whaling. Greenpeace members try to stop Japanese whaling ships from catching whales.

◀ It has been suggested that fishing boats use nets with large holes so that young fish can escape, grow, and breed, and that people stop fishing in places where the fish breed.

Disappearing ice

Not only is polar food disappearing, but so is the ice. People burn lots of oil, gas, and coal, as well as cut down trees. This causes global warming, which means the world is getting warmer, and this makes the ice break up and melt. In the Arctic, this means that polar bears cannot cross the ice to hunt for seals, so they starve to death.

Shrinking ice shelves

The Antarctic has many ice shelves, which are huge masses of ice that float on the water. As the Antarctic becomes warmer, these ice shelves have started to disappear. The Antarctic is shrinking more quickly than people thought.

▼ During the Antarctic summer, some of the ice melts. In recent years, the ice melt has started earlier and more ice is melting.

The ozone layer

Ozone is an invisible gas in the air around us. It protects Earth from the Sun's harmful ultraviolet rays. Over many years ozone has been eaten away by chemicals called chlorofluorocarbons (CFCs) that come from spray cans, air conditioning systems, and refrigerators. The CFCs have made a hole in the ozone layer over the Antarctic, which means harmful rays get through and damage the ground below. This ozone hole is getting bigger and bigger.

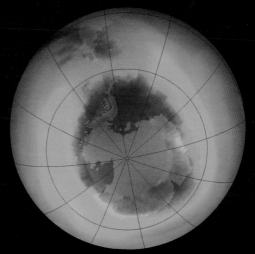

The ozone hole over the Antarctic on September 1, 1985. The hole is colored blue.

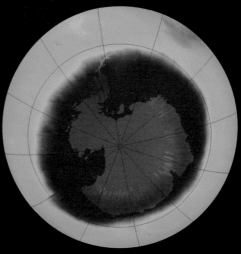

The ozone hole on September 1, 2006.

▲ *Tourists travel across the ice in special snow buggies to watch polar bears. Care is needed to make sure too much tourism doesn't damage the place where the polar bears live.*

The last wilderness

Antarctica is the world's last remaining wilderness. Many countries have signed an agreement to make sure that the Antarctic is never owned by one country and that harmful wastes are never dumped there. Some people want to make sure that, in the future, there is no oil exploration or mining there. It is too precious to spoil.

Facts and Records

Animal Feats

🐾 Each year in March, emperor penguins walk in single file across the ice for more than 62 miles (100 km) to reach their breeding grounds, where there is thicker ice and fewer predators.

🐾 Each year, in Canada, more than 2 million caribou walk from their summer feeding grounds to the northern forests, a journey many hundreds of miles long.

🐾 The Arctic tern makes the longest migration of any bird. It flies more than 21,750 miles (35,000 km) each year— almost the circumference of the earth.

🐾 A pack of wolves consists of between six and eight individuals, but some packs can be as small as two and others as large as 30.

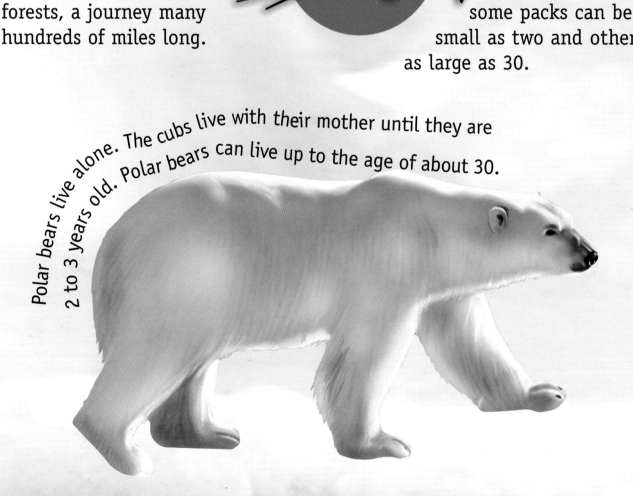

Polar bears live alone. The cubs live with their mother until they are 2 to 3 years old. Polar bears can live up to the age of about 30.

The albatross is one of the biggest flying birds. It weighs about 25 pounds (11 kg).

- Antarctic fish have anti-freeze in their blood and tissues to keep their bodies from freezing.

- The Arctic fox has fur on the bottom of its paws so its feet do not get cold when it runs on the ice and digs holes in the snow.

- Krill is the most common animal in the world's oceans.

- More than 40 different types of birds visit the Antarctic in summer, but only two, the adelie penguin and the emperor penguin, spend the winter there.

- The largest insect that is found living in Antarctica is a wingless midge that is half an inch (12 mm) long.

- Emperor penguins swim at speeds of 6 to 8 miles per hour (10 to 14 kph).

A male walrus can weigh up to 4,000 pounds (1,814 kg).

The average adult emperor penguin is 4 feet (1.3 m) tall and weighs 100 pounds (45 kg).

Polar Facts

- The Arctic Ocean is mainly about 3,280 feet (1,000 m) deep, but in a few places it is almost 18,044 feet (5,500 m) deep. It is covered by ice for most of the year. The ice is about 9.8 feet (3 m) thick, although in some places it is much thicker.

- Due to global warming, the ice over the Arctic Ocean is shrinking by about three percent every year.

- The Arctic is dark from October to February and temperatures can fall as low as –76°F (–60°C). In the middle of summer the Sun never sets, and there is continual daylight.

- The Antarctic is the fifth-largest continent in the world and is twice the size of Australia. The continent was not discovered until 1820.

- At the South Pole, the temperature ranges from –4°F (–20°C) in summer to a very cold –94°F (–70°C) in winter. The strong winds make it feel even colder. It is so cold that if you were to throw a bucket of water into the air, the water would freeze before it hit the ground. Scientists have to wear a face mask so that the air is warmed up before they breathe it in; otherwise, it would freeze their lungs.

- Virtually all of the land in the Antarctic is covered by a thick layer of ice. In some places the ice is 2½ miles (4 km) thick.

- Mountains in the Antarctic have been buried by the ice, and only their tips appear above the ice. The ice is so heavy that it has caused the land to sink below sea level.

- More than two-thirds of the world's freshwater (water we can drink) is locked up in the Antarctic ice.

- Antarctica is the driest continent on Earth. There are dry valleys in the Antarctic, which receive no rain or snow. There are a few plants and some microorganisms in the soil but little else.

Glossary

Owls are predators and need to catch prey to stay alive.

Blizzard A storm with snow and strong winds.

Breed When an animal meets a partner and has babies.

Canine tooth A tooth found near the front of the mouth; the canine tooth is particularly long in predators, such as polar bears.

CFCs This is short for chloro-fluorocarbons, which are chemicals that pass into the air and destroy the ozone layer.

Flippers Animals, such as seals, have flippers instead of legs and feet, and birds, such as penguins, have flippers instead of wings. This is to help them travel quickly and smoothly through the water.

Ice sheet A thick covering of ice over land.

Ice shelf Thick ice that extends from the land over the sea.

Krill A small, shrimplike animal that lives in huge shoals in polar seas.

Predator An animal that hunts other animals for food.

Prey Animals that are hunted as food by other animals.

Scavengers Animals that feed on the remains of other animals.

Shoal A large group of fish or krill.

Tundra A huge, flat, open space without trees.

Tusk An extra-long tooth that sticks out of the side of the mouth when the mouth is closed. A walrus has two tusks, one on either side of its mouth, and narwhals have one long tusk.

Ultraviolet Invisible rays that come from the Sun. They can cause sunburn and damage your skin.

Vibrations Shaking or very fast to-and-fro movements.

Whiskers Thick hairs around the mouth that are very sensitive to touch; used by animals, such as the walrus, to find food on the sea bed.

Index